In My Thoughts

A Handbook For Families
Who Have Lost A Child In Death

Barbara Klich

Bereaved Families Of Ontario, Metropolitan Toronto

IN MY THOUGHTS

Canadian Cataloguing in Publication Data

KLICH, Barbara
        In My Thoughts: A Handbook For Families Who Have Lost A Child In Death

ISBN 0-9699015-0-X

1. Bereavement - Psychological aspects.
2. Children - Death - Psychological aspects.
I. Bereaved Families of Ontario. Metropolitan Toronto. II. Title.

BF575.G7K5 1994 155.9'37   C94-932707-7

IN MY THOUGHTS ...

DEDICATION

*T*his book is dedicated to all of the hearts who have lost a child - the parents, sisters and brothers, grandparents, friends, aunts, uncles, in the hope that they may someday be at peace. It is also meant for others who will see the death of a child from this side of sorrow - doctors, nurses, teachers, guidance counselors, neighbours, and anyone who comes into contact with the bereaved, in the hope that they will understand a little better.

This book is dedicated to my late son, Teddy, who is always in my thoughts.

It is also dedicated to my father, Joseph Daniel McNamara, who told me as he was dying, that I should remember to write my book. I thought, that in his final moments as he battled leukemia, he had mistaken me for my sister Helen, who was writing a book at that time. Now, I think he may have meant me. I hope that *In My Thoughts,* will honour his memory and reflect the values he gave to each of his children and grandchildren.

Teddy, may you rest in peace with Da.

In My Thoughts has been made possible because of my husband Ted, who was always there in the good times and the bad; daughters Julia and Christina and sons Joseph and John, who through the years have helped us all mend a little with joy and laughter as well as pain and sorrow; Joel who joined our family in 1981; and grandchildren Blaise, Caleigh, and Jared, who give us hope for tomorrow.

After Teddy's death, a woman told me that I must remember that life is a tapestry and I was only seeing the broken threads ... someday, I would see the full picture. I know that the missing threads that have been torn away through death are bitter, but they do form the whole picture of life and I am grateful for them.

It has taken almost 19 years to write about my son's death. And it is as difficult today as it would have been had I started to put this book together a week following his death. The hurt is as strong, but time has given me a new strength to make it happen. A man who had lost three children a year before our loss, told me that coping with my son's death would be similar to living with arthritis - it is always there, but some days are better than others. That was good advice. It has taken me on this difficult journey; a journey I would like to share with the reader's permission.

BARBARA KLICH

PREFACE

$\mathcal{A}$ familiar maxim reminds us that 'it is better to light a candle then to curse the darkness' and Barbara Klich's personal story of tragedy lives this theme. In illuminating the darkness and depths of grief, she brings warmth to soothe and heal the broken heart. As she walks us through the aftermath of her son Ted's death, we become part of her journey and get closer to the pain that she experienced. Barbara's commitment to making sense out of that which is totally senseless inspires us and leads us to the hope that she slowly discovered.

This labour of love will undoubtedly give direction to those who are also confronted with walking the path that Barbara knows so well - other bereaved parents. It will speak with resonance and clarity to a wider audience who know about grief, but have not personally lost a child. Thank you, Barbara for *In My Thoughts*.

David Wright, Professional Consultant
Bereaved Families of Ontario - Metropolitan Toronto

IN MY THOUGHTS

TABLE OF CONTENTS

CHAPTER ONE

IF ONLY ...

He had dark eyes, almost black, a handsome young face, a husky build, a love for music, a nature that was gentle in its own way ... he was just coming into his own.

The two words that kept sitting in my head the night that Teddy was killed, and the many days and nights and years that followed ... 'if only' ... over and over again. I would hear myself say 'if only' we had eaten dinner a few minutes earlier or later, that car would not have killed my son; 'if only' his piano lesson had been on a different day of the week, he would be alive; 'if only', 'if only', 'if only', it seemed an endless chant that took me nowhere, but always stayed firmly implanted. It was guilt nipping at my heart and soul. I knew in my mind that no matter how many things may have been different, the end result was the same and because it was a Wednesday night, and because we had eaten at the normal dinner hour, and because we could never change anything that happened on the 22nd day of October, 1975, Ted was dead. And, we were alive.

As any parent who has lost a child, I was in shock when it all happened. Perhaps the reason I kept going over those two words so often was an attempt to lessen the impact and think of some logical explanation that could explain death when it strikes down a child.

The night of October 22, 1975, was pleasant. It was a mild evening, without the bite of autumn and without the heat of summer. It was almost nondescript. Ted was talking to me as I washed the dishes at the sink and explaining his hopes for the future. They sounded so remote - he was going to finish high school, attend university, probably engineering, and then travel all over the world so he could see everything before he settled down. He was 16 and he knew what he wanted! I listened and continued to wash the dishes.

His youngest brother John, who was six years old, played with him and they tussled about on the floor together. At about 6:25 p.m. he left the house, a knapsack on his back filled with his music books and a copy of "The Homecoming" that he was learning to play. It was still light outdoors as the time hadn't changed. I don't know why, but I didn't turn to say good-bye, wish him well in his piano lesson, or even caution him as I usually did. I called "Bye, Ted" and I never saw him again.

He was a young man who loved sports, music, life. He had a spiritual side to him that is not always seen in the young. A few nights earlier he had told me that a priest had visited his school and a religious picture was placed on the stage of the auditorium. He said that he and several of his buddies seemed to think that this picture was looking at him. We laughed and joked about that and wondered why it had happened.

At about 7:40 p.m. a policeman came to my door. I was busy in my downstairs office writing a script that was due the next morning. When my son Joe called to me that a policeman was upstairs, I thought he must be joking. I came up and saw my neighbour whose face was locked in a half smile, half look of terror. I was trying to read what her eyes were telling me, but I couldn't.

"I have bad news for you. Your son Ted is dead."

The words came from the officer in a halting but serious tone. There was no mistake in what he said and he tried to convey that to me.

In a split second, I thought this was absurd. He had the wrong house, the wrong family, the wrong Ted. This wasn't the way things were ever supposed to be - on the radio, on television, in the movies, there was supposed to be music, lights, sirens. There was a muffled scream and I realized that it was from me. I ran to the phone and tried to reach my husband who was at church since this was the anniversary of his mother's death. The janitor who answered the office phone spoke only Polish. I spoke only English. Somehow, I made him understand that he had to go into the church and find my husband. My husband has often said that when he walked into that office and saw the red light flashing on the phone - he thought it must have been a call saying my mother had died. He never suspected it was his son.

I didn't know how to tell him. I simply blurted out that a policeman was standing in the hallway telling me that Teddy was dead. I asked him to meet us at the hospital.

I looked frantically for my purse and called the children. My neighbour asked me why I needed a purse. I looked at her and thought that if a mistake had been made, Teddy and I would have to take a taxi back home - he may have been hurt and I would need money for the ride.

I told my son Joe who was 11 that our neighbour would stay with him and the younger children and I would call him as soon as I could.

The police officer escorted me to the cruiser and we slowly drove to the hospital. There were few words and a wall of silence seemed to exist - the policeman appeared uneasy, I had no idea what to say. When we arrived at the hospital, a nurse met us and directed us to a little room. She said that I would have to go to the morgue and identify my son. We walked down a staircase and along a corridor. The door opened slightly and I saw his jeans - his legs looked as though they had been burned. My eyes stopped halfway as I scanned his legs. I told the nurse I could not go in. I closed my eyes and said I would wait for my husband. Somehow, we were in her office once again and I phoned a relative asking that our daughter, who was on a school trip in Quebec, be contacted. I then called a priest.

I spoke without a break in my voice and there were no tears. Inside, there was an explosion - an emotional concussion, and yet my outer being was as calm as a quiet sea.

This has stayed with me - everyone reacts so differently. My nature, for whatever reason, didn't scream or shout, but that didn't mean I wasn't hurting. I was in shock in my own way.

4

If there is a lesson to be learned, it is never to judge the bereaved; for each person will react differently. Because you don't see the tears, it doesn't mean they are not there.

My husband and father-in-law arrived at the hospital and together we walked down to the morgue. My husband went into the room. My father-in-law entered the room; I stood in the hallway. I can still hear the shrieks as my father-in-law saw his eldest grandson. I have often felt it was a terrible mistake to have allowed him to see Teddy. My father-in-law had suffered the loss of his wife just one year earlier and he should have been spared this as well. Now, as a grandparent myself, I can only respect him and the way he handled life after that day. But I do feel that it must have been difficult.

I hugged the wall as I heard the cries and I wanted to disappear from the face of the earth.

In our own experience, the breaking of news was in some ways brutal and so direct. Perhaps, there was no other way. I think the police must have a terrible time trying to choose the 'best' way of telling someone that a child has died. Sometimes, I think there is no right way and there is no wrong way ... it just happens.

I do think that hospital personnel must be better trained. I hope today this is the case. I had the distinct feeling that the nurses and the one doctor I saw wanted me out of that hospital because, after all, Teddy was dead and nothing more could be done for him. Death defeats the purpose of a hospital where healing and health should be restored.

5

Something can be done for the bereaved however - a kind word, an arm around the shoulder, a moment of silence together.

If there is a need in today's hospitals I think it has to be volunteers who can sit for a moment and console the bereaved. Blessed are they who console, because the impact of a death is such that the initial first moments are recorded in your heart forever. I know it is difficult and I know that hospitals can't do everything, but even if there had been one person who could have sat for a moment without getting on with the official business of the day, it would have been appreciated.

We were asked where we would like the body sent and I guess at that moment I snapped a little. "Damn it, " I thought, "this is not a body, this is my son, how dare anyone refer to him like that."

We were told that an autopsy would have to be performed since he had been killed on a road and this would be done with or without our permission. He had been riding a moped that had a governor on it that didn't allow his exceeding a certain speed. He was about eighteen inches from the curb when a car coming in the opposite direction crossed three lanes of traffic and hit him head on. The moped's gas tank exploded on impact, and he was hurled several feet into a ravine area. We were told that he had probably suffered broken legs (his riding boots had been thrown off in the explosion), internal injuries and severe head injuries, even though he had been wearing a helmet. The coroner would have to give us a report. We should prepare for his funeral and let the hospital know which funeral director would pick him up.

We left the hospital with the priest who had come as soon as we called. At the accident scene, my husband insisted on getting out of the car. There was little to see other than tire marks. The priest, who is a still a good friend, spoke softly about Teddy and talked with my husband at the site. Then, he came back to the car and he said - "You can't fault the lad!"

For whatever reason, those words were right for the moment and have stayed with me.

Many times, I have experienced tremendous waves of guilt over Teddy's death. And, then I would think about it ... he was in the curb lane, he was not speeding, he had no escape, another cyclist a few feet away narrowly missed being hit, there was no explanation for the car's moving in and hitting him. He was not at fault and we were not at fault, and yet a parent always feels that the child is to be protected and therefore, anything that happens is the parent's fault. It was not an emotion that I could escape.

The only words that brought me back to some sanity were those of the priest - "You can't fault the lad!" Perhaps we cannot fault ourselves, although we often do.

Dealing with the guilt is difficult and I am sure every parent has to come through this in different ways. I can only say that time is one method of healing, and the realization that there are some things we can never change, no matter what we do or say.

Back at home that evening, some of the family had gathered. My sister Helen made a pot of tea. Neighbours who had heard about the accident came to the door, and for the next few days there was an outburst of kindness from so many people. I will always be grateful to everyone in that community who brought not only food and flowers, but also kind words and their own memories.

When everyone had left the house and the children were in bed, and our daughter Julia had been informed and was making arrangements to get back from Quebec, I sat in the living room in the dark. It would have been wrong somehow to have had the lights turned on, I thought. I wanted to run as far as I could from this monster of death that had robbed us this night of our son. I wanted to wrestle death to the ground and stick a huge sword through its throat, I wanted to stop it from ever touching another young life. I sat paralyzed with fear, anger, grief, hurt, guilt - only my eyes moved.

We were able to get through the next few days and I still wonder how this was ever accomplished. Our two older children Julia and Joe accompanied my husband Ted and me to the funeral home where we chose a coffin. Can you imagine shopping for a coffin - this one versus this one, I couldn't believe I was really there. We talked briefly about the funeral, the viewing, the cemetery. We were told we would have to make the arrangements at the cemetery right away and I thought that there would have to be sufficient space for me since I wanted to jump into that hole in the ground as well.

We were told that it would be best to have a closed coffin and simply place Ted's school portrait on top.

He would be placed in a shroud rather than dressed because of his injuries.

On that first afternoon, streams of young men in their school uniforms came to the funeral home. My mother sat and watched them pass the coffin in their blue blazers and grey flannels, the same outfit Teddy had often worn. She couldn't move a muscle, she just stared; and quietly some of the young men, sensing her grief, came over and introduced themselves. These young gentlemen, who had so often joked and danced in our home, were now etched in a grief that was not appropriate for the young. They looked tormented and hurt and angry. They should have been out on a football field or at a concert, but certainly never in a funeral home. Some came over to me and laughed about the good times they had enjoyed with Ted; others were too overcome to say a word.

I think I learned then that in death we don't change our personalities, but we do take on another aspect of ourselves. One young man stood tearfully at the coffin and said nothing. Later, another friend told me that Ted had defended him when others had made fun of him, and he was too upset to say anything.

Friends poured into the house with food and books and gifts,

9

and I learned quickly that as a bereaved parent you must understand that not everyone will say something that is tactful, consoling, or even smart. One woman asked why I had not insisted the coffin be open, and I explained that he had been badly burned and injured. Still she carried on and said we were wrong and we should have not denied everyone the right of seeing Teddy for the last time so people could remember what he looked like.

"I'm his Mother, for God's sake, how could I ever forget him?" I shouted in my head in silence.

But, I smiled and said yes, you are probably right.

In the days that followed, I agonized that in 20 years time I may indeed not remember him and then what would I ever do ... could I always recall his smile, his eyes, his face. Soon after, I arranged with an artist to paint a portrait taken from his photos, and today, 19 years later, I know that with or without the portrait, I still see every line, every feature that made him so special.

The funeral was difficult - there were so many of his friends in their school uniforms, our daughter Julia's friends in their uniforms, the neighbours and relatives, so many people. We followed the coffin down the aisle and a friend played the organ - it was music from *Swan Lake* which Teddy had been studying and had played in the drum corps. There was a sea of faces, an altar filled with flowers, and a coffin. An honour guard of young men and women from the two drum corps he had marched with escorted his body from the church. At the cemetery another friend in military uniform gave a final salute. The young men and women of that day will always stand out in my memory as the very best when they put everything aside and came to say farewell to a friend and to console his family.

A gentle rain sprinkled over the lowered coffin and I felt that my heart would break into a thousand pieces and scatter into the dust of time.

At home, and it is a modest house, there were so many people I wondered where everyone could possibly stand. Friends had already started to prepare food and drinks for the crowd. Some of his close friends asked if they could go to his room and listen to music. They leafed through his albums and then looked through the scrap books of the De La Salle Drum Corps tours and the Crusaders and reminisced about their great times together.

People spilled into the yard, the basement rec room, the main floor, the kitchen. Everyone had that look that this was somehow the wrong picture ... it was a funeral for someone who should have been as alive and vibrant as his friends.

Some of our friends stood by and had a troubled look, as though death could hit them next. Some appeared anxious, as though they had to leave because the angel of death might strike their children as well.

The pall bearers were together in the kitchen - his uncles Stan and Joe, his principal "Uncle Normie", his friends, Mike,

11

Mark, John, Mark, and Tom. Coming to terms with death must have been difficult for the young men who had laughed with him a few days earlier and had now escorted his body to the graveside. His friend Mike just put his arm around me and didn't say a word. We did communicate through our silence.

Another friend Mark kept busy arranging things and when our eyes met, we both cried a little. The scars are very deep when one of tender years dies and the hurt lasts such a long time. I was so thankful though that these young people were with us to keep some of Teddy alive in this initial period of mourning.

When the last guest had left the house, and the dishes had been cleared, and the flowers arranged in place, my husband and I stared into space.

A vase with a single rose stood on the piano beside his music - it had been sent by the organist and his wife. The rose looked perfect. It was for a young man who had been perfect, a young man who had had everything in life waiting for him.

There are no lessons for those who are bereaved or for those who want to console the bereaved, because no textbook could ever tell anyone what to expect, consider, even know, or do. Things just seem to happen. If those who comfort can be quiet at times, be kind, place an arm around the shoulder, allow the tears to flow and not try to stem them with empty words, then blessed are those who comfort.

We will always remember in detail the events of that week when the days of our beloved Teddy ended.

He had dark eyes, almost black, a handsome young face, a husky build, a love for music, a nature that was gentle in its own way... and he never came into his own.

In My Thoughts

CHAPTER TWO

DEATH HAS NO FEELINGS

$\mathcal{F}$or whatever reason, I guess most of us feel that death is the normal result of having lived for many years, and a natural end to our days. When death strikes down a child however, it is quite unnatural and certainly not normal. It is always unexpected, it is always somehow outside the realm of our understanding.

It was the morning of his life...

I said that I acted in an outwardly calm manner when I learned of Teddy's death, but I was really undergoing a war in my head. My heart was shattering, but my head was telling me to carry on with the things that had to be completed. My heart knew that things were wrong, but my head couldn't understand.

Shock seems to set in and we go on automatic pilot when something as strange as the death of a child happens.

And when you think about it, this must be a rather normal response. I was angry that something as insidious as death could have overpowered my son who was young, vibrant, and strong. He had never been ill, he was fit, he could out wrestle his friends, so there was no logic to this death, which had cut him down.

As well, I found that I was resentful ... why hadn't he had a death that would have given us some time to show him our love, our attention, our caring? I felt that those parents who had watched over their dying children through an illness must have been blessed.

Then, as the years passed and I spoke with other parents, I wondered if we had been spared terrible times by not seeing his suffering. This is often a quandary. I don't think there is any answer that can help the bereaved parent who has seen a child die in any way.

I remember sitting up in an arm chair for many nights and trying to reconstruct the accident. Had he been unconscious immediately? What were his last thoughts as he saw that car? Did he see the car or was everything so swift that it was just a streak of fire and it was over? Was there pain or was life sucked away in moments?

A few months after his death, I went into hospital for the day to have my wisdom teeth removed. I was given an injection and then a mask was placed over my face. Everything suddenly went black. I awoke several hours later and there was no one in the room. I looked at my hands that were a light blue in colour. I wondered if I was alive and I actually hoped that I too had died. Then, a nurse came by and said I had suffered a hemorrhage and was doing well at this point.

That blackness stayed with me, as I wondered more and

more about that final moment Teddy must have experienced. I will never know, of course, but these thoughts and images haunted me for years. However, it isn't wise to focus only on the last moments for long periods of time because it is a form of self-torment. I have tried in a positive way to think about the great times we had together, the summer vacations, the Christmas holidays, the family dinners, the times his friends came to our house when they were on tour with the drum corps, all of the happy moments we spent together.

On Mother's Day when Teddy was about 11, he bought me a package of seeds and made a tiny wooden box for them - the cosmos that grew from those seeds are still in the garden and their seeds have spread to neighbouring yards. I have often wondered if he would enjoy the fact that so many years later his cosmos are in full bloom in the area. These and many more are the memories I cherish, and they are the ones that help in the healing.

And it is here that it is important for those who want to comfort or even show their sympathy to know that this child who has died is still very much alive in the family's mind. Many people say they simply do not know what to say to a bereaved family. I think that it is very important that the child be remembered. If a parent wants to talk about the great marks that the child achieved at school, or the instrument she played in the school orchestra, or the ambitions that were never realized, please allow them to do this. Many people unwittingly try to erase the memory of the dead child as though that person had never existed. This is very painful for any parent or brother or sister.

One woman told me that she hadn't spoken of Teddy because she was afraid I might cry. Well, if he wasn't worth my tears, what value is there in life...of course, we may cry, but we may benefit, and those who speak with us may also benefit from tears.

Many bereaved parents complain of sleeping problems - nightmares, insomnia, sleeping all of the time. I must have been terribly tired in those first weeks, but sleep did not come easily and when it did it was only for short periods of time. It may be necessary to seek professional medical help because these patterns can get out of hand. For some people working until fatigue dictates sleep may help.

There are no right or wrong answers in any of this and it is important to treat yourself as an individual and not rely on accounts from other people. Some people appear to benefit from medications, but it is important to always consult with a physician in this area as some people in grief are susceptible to problems that can arise from sleeping pills, alcohol, or other addictions.

I think that I wanted to be fully alert at all times, I wanted answers to his death, I wanted to know that everything was being handled properly, and as a result I shunned any suggestions that sedatives could help me. I was never hysterical, but there were many times when I truly felt that I could not continue to carry on. Somehow an inner strength kept pushing just a little so that I didn't give up or give in.

Many have said that there are steps to the grief process and I think that perhaps this is true. I don't think, however, that the steps have to come in any order, that all steps have to be experienced, and that there is a textbook approach to grief. Certainly, some time in the grief process one may experience shock, which can last from a few moments to weeks on end. You simply feel that nothing that has happened can be true, you have trouble relating to life around you, you are numb.

Everyone reacts in a different way and some people simply withdraw and do not want to talk to others, even to their own families. Others can't stop talking and they must say the child's name over and over in conversation, even with strangers, in an attempt to keep at least the memory alive. It becomes a mantra and it can in some cases, soothe the breaking heart.

Emotions can run from intense anger to guilt. The anger can be quite irrational and directed at almost everyone - at the police who should have prevented such an accident, at society that is so fast-paced that everyone has to get from A to B quickly, at doctors who could not help the child or find a cure, at other young people who are still alive, at God who has forsaken us by allowing a young person to die at this tender age.

There is guilt, as I have mentioned earlier, and sometimes it is shifted to others - your spouse, your relatives, the friends of the dead child, but then it always returns to you, the parent.

There is hurt that cuts right through the human heart and makes one feel that life is so senseless and useless.

There is frustration and hopelessness and the sense that none of this really ever happened.

Sometimes, more than one emotion can hit and there is tremendous confusion that rips the mind apart.

I think that it is important for friends and relatives and co-workers to realize that just because a child has died, that child is not to be immediately forgotten. The child was a part of the family's life for many years and the child is still a part of the family, but in a different way.

Many people would meet me at work or on the street and talk in a forced way about everything from the weather to the hockey game - both topics I had no reason to discuss. If I tried to steer the conversation in the direction of my son, they would edge away, sometimes quite visibly upset, and either leave or once again talk about something else. In those first days following his death, I remember few people who actually spoke with me about my son's death ... there was always avoidance.

I do remember though one acquaintance, and in other times we had joked and laughed about our respective children. He didn't know that Teddy had died and he asked what was the matter since I wasn't my usual self. I explained what had happened and instead of moving the conversation away, he asked about my son. He asked me about Teddy! He actually listened and never tried to abandon the subject. I spilled out a lot of words that day and we laughed and reminisced. Later, I learned that he too had lost a child many years before.

He never mentioned this; but from his own memories of sorrow, he was able to reach out.

I also recall a man who had been a friend for many years, who said that after all, I had other children, so that was good. I looked at him and didn't say a word, but in my mind I was cursing such stupidity and asking if I had lost one finger in an accident, and I still had four left, would I be the same? The special place that each child has is important and cannot be replaced.

Another friend said that I was still young after all, and could have another child. Again, I felt that these people were looking at the death of a child as so much inventory and if one was lost on the way, a replacement could be on order.

Although each may have been well intentioned, these comments stayed with me for many years and I would hope that people are a little more careful in their words to the bereaved.

One comment came from a neighbour who was in her late teens. She was working in the local supermarket and she stopped to talk to me. She said that she was sad to hear of Teddy's death, but, perhaps that was his destiny. I thought that for someone so young she was making sense. It is something I have pondered over the years and it has become a way of accepting such a tragedy.

In our case, our son's death or destiny had resulted from a traffic accident. It was sudden, brutal, shocking.

One night when I was sitting in a semi-stupor in the late autumn, I thought about all of the parents who have experienced the deaths of their children. My mind turned to the horrible deaths we often see reported in the media and I wondered how parents ever cope with these tragedies.

Children who have been murdered, who have died from lingering illnesses, who have been in accidents, who have suffered with AIDS, children who have committed suicide, children who are the victims of starvation, war, atrocities ... I thought that each must have had their own special kind of Hell. A parent cannot help thinking of the moments when the child is near death and there is no one to help.

I thought about those parents who may have had children who were never accepted because of disabilities or mental illness; and I wondered how they coped with the death of these children - in some cases, relatives and friends may see that type of a death as a blessing. But for a parent losing a child is still the same, no matter what. I recall a family who had a son who was in a wheelchair most of his young life. He couldn't speak, move his body, or indicate in any way that he was absorbing anything that was going on.

I think he did understand, and he looked in the most gentle

24

and loving way at his mother. When he died, his parents had a look of desperation. I have often wondered how his family recovered. For anyone to have seen the young man as only a burden is not to have seen the love that came from his eyes.

We have become accustomed to resolving all of life's problems, tragedies, and events, in a thirty-minute package. We live according to the gospel of the soundbite; society and even community values have imposed this upon us. Grief cannot be dealt with through egg timers that tell us when we should cry, stop crying, smile, frown. Grief has its own timetable and it varies with each person.

We never know how we will react to any situation and in death this still holds true. I have spoken with bereaved families and heard that for months following the death of a child, these people would do strange things - one woman said she played the violin for hours every day and never cleaned her house or attended to her family; another said that she became compulsive in exercise and walking, and it wasn't until she was truly exhausted one day that she realized she was really trying to walk away her grief. A father said that he decided to dig up his yard and he kept thinking that he should have buried his son in the yard where he could be with him; he said he attacked the ground with a viciousness he hadn't realized was in him. Some have said that they simply withdrew and refused to talk to anyone or answer a phone; others ate or drank or smoked, perhaps in an attempt to bring themselves closer to death. While many of these patterns sound very strange and counter-productive, they can be therapeutic in the short run. Obviously, if they go on for long periods of time and if there is a danger in them, they should be stopped and counselling should be initiated. Pathological grief needs professional counselling, but sometimes determining what is pathological can be difficult.

For those who have not experienced the death of a child, judging what is a normal time frame is very difficult. Perhaps, too often physicians will suggest that the recovery is not fast enough, perhaps they should realize that recovery is an inoperative word and healing will take much longer than most physical ailments.

Coming through the channel of darkness that is the death of a child is never easy and there is no formula that will make things right.

For many, though, special bereavement counselling groups can be of immense help. Speaking with other parents whose children have died may relieve some of the pressures that can make parents feel they are alone. Only in discussing with others, can we see that death does hit our children and we are not alone when it happens to us.

It was the darkness of our being.

In My Thoughts

CHAPTER THREE

HE WAS MY BROTHER ...

*T*he family unit is important in today's society, especially when everything around us is breaking down. However, when we strive to keep things together, and death butts its head into our being, how can we ever cope as a family again?

> *Every child has a place in the week of our family...*
> *Friday's child is loving and giving.*

In every family, there will always be disagreements, petty jealousies, fights, jokes played on one another, all of the points and counterpoints that contribute to our individual selves. The birth order can also be significant and we often hear people talking about the oldest child who is a little more sensitive and responsible as opposed to the middle child who is often caught between with fewer responsibilities and fewer privileges, and the youngest child who seems in some cases to be able to get away with a little more because he or she has learned from the others.

When that family pattern is broken through the death of a child, everything seems to fall into turmoil. The next child may be expected to take the place of the child who has died and this can be a difficult, if not impossible, task.

Sometimes, the parents are not even aware that this is happening - a son has died and the next son immediately feels that he must take on the chores that were his brother's responsibility. He may also want to take on far more than he can handle and if there is a significant age difference, problems will arise. Other children in the family may decide that they will have to do certain things and may not even consult with the parents who may be thinking that they will work on those tasks in memory of the child who has died.

Chaos can result and life is not only on the edge because of the shock of the death, but because all of these different feelings are coming to the fore.

Sorting out the roles can be painful.

Explaining death to a young child is difficult because no one wants to frighten. At the same time, the reality is there and the youngster has to know that the brother or sister has died and will not be returning to the house.

How do you explain death to a four year old?

On the day of the funeral, we were trying to get everyone ready. Our four year old Christina, said she didn't have any shoes. She looked at me when she said this and I became agitated. Why was this child saying something so foolish - of course she had shoes, she had new black patent leather shoes, she had school shoes, she had all kinds of shoes. She finally found one shoe and said that the other must be lost. It was getting closer to the time that the limo would be picking us up. In a distorted and silly moment, I thought of her with only one shoe and I could see Teddy smiling at her and making a joke. I started to laugh at the whole scene and then caught myself. Eventually, we found her other shoe and we were able to leave the house properly attired. It wasn't until months later that I realized she may have been afraid to go to the church for the funeral and she had lost her shoe on purpose. There are so many instances of little things that went on in those days that we failed to see at the time.

I guess that I wasn't much help in explaining what had happened to Teddy, because one evening about a week after his death, I overheard this same child ask her brother who was about six, what it meant when someone died, and she asked where Teddy was ... her brother said that he had died and his body was no longer in Downsview, but his soul was always with us. She said okay, and was satisfied. Why had I not been able to explain things that well? Perhaps, because I was trying to protect her innocence, trying to say something that would not contribute to more questions, trying to save myself from something I didn't even understand. I know that from the mouths of babes we often find wisdom.

When children return to school following the death of a sibling, it can be very difficult. There are now support teams in many schools that will help children and their friends when death robs them of a student. When Teddy died, we had only ourselves and the good graces of the teachers and principals to help. I will always be indebted to the principal of my older daughter's high school who took her out for breakfast one day and just listened to her talk about her brother. Julia and Teddy were only 14 months apart in age and his death was not only that of a brother, but also a buddy who shared the same friends, interests, ideas. Julia had been busy helping us, we hadn't really helped her. Sister Philomena did that and we will always be grateful because she treated Julia, not as a student, but as an adult who needed some quiet conversation.

The other children were in elementary school when Teddy died and generally the teachers were in tune with them when they returned to school.

I do remember one teacher, though, who talked about grades and classroom performance at a parents' night about a year after his death. She seemed to avoid any mention of Teddy and I asked if his death had impacted on the child's school work. She looked at me and said that she, too, had a lost a brother when she was young in a similar way. And, she said that it was important that we not tie the other children down and restrict everything they wanted to do because that can have a terrible effect on them. She said quietly that life had been difficult for her because her parents became overly protective. I always remembered her words, but more than the words, I remembered her eyes that were so deep and so sad. I vowed then that to the best of my ability I would try to make the lives of the children as normal as possible. This hasn't been the case entirely though and I have suggested to them that there are some things they are better off not doing when the element of danger is so great they could be hurt or killed. Some have not been happy with me over this.

I know that lightning isn't supposed to strike twice, but I have talked with families who have lost two and even three children. I can't control death, but I sure hope I can caution my own children about it.

Not all students will be kind, though, and children will say terrible things simply because they are children. It is difficult for youngsters to be singled out in a crowd, when other children refer to them as the "guy whose brother got killed", mixed reactions can result. Some children may fight, may get their anger out by acting up in school, by not paying attention, by being the class clown. Teachers should be watchful and realize that the student who was progressing well before the death of a sibling, but now has problems, may need some special attention. Much will depend on the age of the child and it is probably not a good idea to 'baby' or favour a child with special treatment. I feel that to single out a child who is in grief is not the proper way to follow through in a classroom, but rather to have a class discussion that may help to explain what bereavement is all about.

Sometimes through drawings, children can express their own inner feelings and how they are coping with the death. I remember speaking with a woman whose child drew pictures of water covering everyone after his sister had died in a drowning accident. What he wasn't talking about, he was feeling and expressing through his art.

Music is another vehicle that can bring out the emotions that may be hiding.

I remember one child who was angry with one of mine and said that he was happy Teddy had died. My child came home very upset, and when we talked about this, I simply said that this was probably just a way the child was trying to make him angry and that the boy didn't really mean anything by it. It was best to forget what had been said and start the new day in a fresh way.

In the family it is very difficult when a child dies. The kitchen table now has an empty chair at it, the child's bedroom still has the bed, dresser, books and records scattered about, the clothes are still in the closet. Everything is the same, but the child is missing. Without thinking, someone says - what will Teddy think about this, or I think I should make his favourite pie tonight and a flood of tears and pent-up emotions can hit.

It is difficult for children to deal with the myriad of emotions that come crashing down. Why are the parents talking so much about Teddy when my report card just came in and I have top marks? Doesn't anyone around here remember that I'm still alive? Am I so worthless they can't even mention my name sometimes? The dead child was not a saint! It is important that the living children realize that love is universal and each is loved in a special way. In the first throes of grief, when a mother cannot hug the dead child, words are often embellished to make him or her seem more important. In time, we all come to terms with our losses and with the gifts that we still have and must cherish. But in the interim, there can be emotional earthquakes.

In any family there can be confusion - I came from a family of five children with four daughters. I think I must have been at least eight years old before I realized my name was really Barbara ... often my mother would say, "HelenMariePeggyBarbara" before she got to me. I found I often did the same thing, calling Teddy by other names and we would laugh about it. After his death, I called one of my children Teddy by mistake and there was a silence in the room that cut right through us. I wasn't sure if I would cry or laugh -I opted for the latter and said I was sorry. There was an outburst of relief and everyone quietly went about their business again.

Sometimes, we expect too much from the children who are left after one dies. We are always comparing them, saying that the deceased child had good grades, was smart, was handsome, and we are comparing him to the others. I probably did this, and I was wrong. However, I am not perfect; and in later years, I realized that this too was a natural happening.

It is important to realize that the children in a family in which a sibling has died are experiencing tremendous insecurity. They ask if they will die as suddenly as their brother. If the child has died from an illness they often ask if they too will develop that disease and die. If it has been a murder, they feel especially vulnerable. No matter how death strikes, it also leaves its shadow on the brothers and sisters who are concerned that because it has hit home, it could hit them as well.

And while childhood should be a time of happy moments, death can shatter the whole image. In our case, our children saw a grandmother die in 1974, a brother in 1975, a grandfather in 1976, and a young uncle in 1979. There was a fear whenever the phone rang late at night that once again death was calling.

Almost one year after Teddy's death, a police car was parked in front of our house. Two officers were inside discussing some of the details of the case involving his accident. My daughter had been out and when she came home and saw the police cruiser, she could not come into the house because she thought that once again, something terrible must have happened. The terror of once again losing someone had a devastating effect on her that evening. She said she relived the night of October 22, 1975.

Preparing children for death is a terrible task and I have spoken with parents who have said that telling their children that a brother or sister has died was a most difficult part of their experience. They wanted to protect the other children. It is probably best to be straightforward and know that honesty does not offer any hope that a mistake has been made. It is important to be there to answer questions the other children may have and to be direct with them. There are of course questions that are difficult to answer. I remember that a few days after the funeral one of the children asked if things could be different would we want to have Teddy back with us.

What a question - of course we would, but we couldn't change anything and as the young woman in the supermarket had said, it was his destiny. We had to accept his death and move on with good memories and positive steps.

Although we never said anything about following in his footsteps or trying to carry out things that Teddy had wanted to do, there seems to be, as we look back, a feeling that each child in the family has worked hard to get through grief. I think that each has been a special monument to Teddy's memory.

When Julia had her first child, a boy, she looked at me and cried. It was then that I think she truly felt the impact of another human life. There are no doubts in my mind that she was devastated by Teddy's death, but the birth of her own child brought it home. She simply asked through her tears ... how we had ever lived through it all.

From the depths of sorrow, there can be positive elements, and I find that every once in a while each child shows something a little special. Each has responded over the years to friends' losses of brothers and sisters by talking and spending time with them. Because they have lived through tremendous grief and loss, they have become a little more attuned to the feelings of others.

Some children will not give any outward signs of sorrow, but through little acts of kindness will show the world that they too have been touched. It is important to realize that every person reacts differently and the quiet ones have their own way of dealing with grief in a continuing fashion through the years.

Young people do want to help and they want to show families they care. I think it is important that they do this in their own way. We were very fortunate that Teddy had so many friends. In December, a few months after his death, his school had a special assembly and we were invited. They dedicated it to his memory and an opera singer was invited to sing along with the choir. It was a moving and magnificent performance as his teachers sang, some with tears standing in their eyes, and remembered him.

The summer after his death, his drum corps dedicated an evening performance to him and his silent tympani stood on the field by itself. The young men and women who had toured and played with him only a year before now played a selection of his favourite music.

In some families, there will be children who naturally have more in common with one another and they tend to stick together, especially in a tragedy. There are also loners who want to be on their own and work out their feelings. There are those who prefer to discuss their ambitions with friends and leave the family out of things. At some point, though, they all do come together for birthdays, holidays, family gatherings, and this is often a time of great uneasiness. One doesn't care for the way another handles grief ... one laughs, one cries. One is a smart guy with lots of jokes; another feels offended that anything funny should even be said at such a time. The parents may be the referees and may become too involved or not involved enough. Of course, as the years pass and everyone matures, things will change and the hurts of yesterday will be less.

For some children, reaching out is difficult and there may be a need for counselling, special attention, or even a pet who can help get the child over the rough times. Sometimes having an animal to care for and to walk with will help work out the kinks of misery that can be deep-seated. For others there is a feeling that never again will that child be close to anyone or anything because death may separate once more.

Certainly, bereavement counselling is important because many young people feel that this has only happened to them and no one else understands. It is only when they have come to see that other people their own age - their own peers - are going through similar feelings that they can come out of their shell. There is always the potential for problems with young people who may be exposed today to so many elements - drugs, alcohol, antisocial behaviour. It is so important that they be helped in a time of grief. Through organizations such as Bereaved Families of Ontario, some of the healing can begin.

I think that it is important to be honest with the young - the pain they feel immediately will be hard to understand, but the pain down the road may be worse. I know that I found that with the passage of weeks, months, years, I was still in pain and I am sure that the young also felt this way.

They can expect denial, shock, depression, confusion, anger, and guilt in the death of a sibling. They need help and healing with each phase of their recovery from the death.

They should know that it is not wrong to laugh and joke about the person just as you cry and feel lost without him or her.

It is important to know that the hurt will go away, but not until time and growth have taken over.

Every child has a place in the week of our family ... Friday's child was loving and giving.

In My Thoughts

CHAPTER FOUR

IT CAN'T HAPPEN TO ME

$\mathcal{H}$earing about the death of a young person is something that had always bothered me. How could this happen? I often thought it must be that something was just plain wrong with the world. But, I thought, it can't happen to me ... I do all of the right things - go to church, don't drink, don't smoke, pay my bills, and live in a nice, smug little existence.

You think you are an island... alone in a sea of desolation.

On the afternoon of October 22, 1975, I had decided to go shopping. I was tired of working and always facing deadlines. I enjoyed my work, but as with everything we become stale and tired and want a few changes. I thought that an afternoon spent shopping might be a pleasant relief. Now, I believe they call this 'retail therapy.' I had been out of sorts for about a week and I had no idea why. Life was fine...the family was healthy, things were going quite well, but for whatever reason, I simply felt 'down.' I wondered weeks later if I was somehow aware in my subconscious that something was going to happen and I was preparing myself. I certainly had no inkling though at the time.

I went shopping and bought a few bolts of wallpaper for a room I was going to brighten up in my spare time. I enjoyed a quick lunch at a fast food restaurant and I came home thinking that now perhaps I would get down to work after dinner. Dinner was another problem ... I really didn't feel like cooking. We would have something from a take out restaurant for a change. I knew that Teddy had to go to his piano lesson after dinner, Julia was away on a school trip to Quebec, my husband would be having dinner with his father, and the younger children always liked fast food if they could get it.

The evening was starting to pick up and once the dishes were cleared and Teddy was on his way to his piano lesson, I decided to get down to the work I had been putting off for a day.

Then, life changed.

That night I learned that no matter what you plan in life, what your priorities are, nothing really matters if your child has died.

I had been living in a cloak of security because everyone was so healthy. I remember talking to women who had children who had been born with serious problems, had developed illnesses, had trouble throughout their young lives, and I had always felt that we were indeed lucky. I had had five pregnancies that had resulted in five healthy children. I knew from speaking with other women how they had mourned their miscarriages, from women who had lost children to crib death and how horrible this must have been, from a woman whose child was killed in front of her eyes when a car went out control, from a lady whose son had died in Europe in wartime and she had to dig his grave all by herself.

These things had not happened to me and so, although they were important and I felt for these families, I didn't really understand how deep their wounds really were since they were not my wounds.

In the days and months after Teddy's death, I often thought about my own life at his age when he died. When I was 16, I remember well the principal at high school coming into the class and telling us that one of our classmates, whose name was also Teddy, had died the night before. The principal left the room and we sat and looked at one another. I couldn't believe that this student who had been sitting next to me the day before was now dead. This was as close as I had come to the death of a young person. My own father had died when I was in my twenties, and a great uncle died in my arms a few years later, but these were deaths that seemed to be in order when we thought about life. A child's death has no order and it is totally out of place.

The manner in which we react to death is difficult to predict. I found that I wanted to talk about my son to everyone I met. I soon learned that people were not interested. When I returned to work for the first time after his death, a co-worker said that I should concentrate on the job and not think too much of Teddy because this would be much healthier. I was very angry and I wanted to shout - "How the hell would you know, since your son is alive and well and waiting for you at home at night." But, I smiled. Someone else said that it is very important to keep busy because otherwise, thoughts will ramble in the head. How absurd, I thought ... these are not ramblings, they are organized and important and must be kept alive or I will lose him again if I lose him in my head.

I was fortunate though because the producer with whom I worked at the CBC was not only kind and understanding, but he sensed when I needed some time away, just to think. It is important for employers to understand the severity of grief in the workplace and to realize that employees will be different following the death of a child. Circumstances vary and many people depend on the job not only for financial needs, but also for some return to stability in their lives.

I did work and I did come home and do the things that had to be done. The meals still had to be prepared, the laundry had to be done, the ironing, the shopping, the banking, the cleaning. There was no escape from any of these things. Yet there had to be time out for grief. I had to find the moments when I could think about what had happened. Usually that time came late at night when the house was quiet and everyone else was asleep. I would think such strange thoughts ... about all of the people who had died through the centuries ... how could there be a place such as Heaven, how many people could be there, was there an afterlife? How could we ever know if Teddy was all right or if he was caught in some halfway house between life and death? Was his soul in this very room, what about the strange things that could happen when people said they knew someone was still near even though that person had died? Grief was making me think that I was indeed losing my mind!

One night I was so totally confused I thought I was going mad. I was sure that if my doctor had come into the room, he would have said, "Okay, Barbara, we will just take you away for a little while and get your head fixed."

Then I looked out of the living room window. There must have been a million stars in the sky and I suddenly thought ... there must be as many stars in that galaxy as there are people who have died over the centuries and each star has its place ... without each star the night would not be as beautiful. For whatever reason, I felt better and I was able to sleep without any terrible dreams that night.

Some people react to death with compulsive behaviour - they want to change themselves by losing weight, looking better, learning something new. Some want to fulfill a death wish by gaining weight, eating, starving themselves, smoking, drinking. Some put aside their grief and say they will deal with it later when the time is right. One man told me that he placed his grief away in a corner of his head. Every so often he visits that corner and then he closes it down again and won't go back because it is too painful. I think I tried to put my grief away like that but it kept coming back and nagging at me. I was a walking wound and every time I bumped into another emotion, there was some bleeding, infection, scarring. I couldn't escape.

Many years later, after my nephew died, my sister would phone me in the middle of the night and sob uncontrollably. She would always apologize for calling at such an hour and then preface her comments with "You have been through it and you have survived, you are the only person I can talk to about this."

I never felt adequate though, because each grief is so special in its way. She had lost her only child and she, too, thought she must be losing her mind. She had trouble sleeping, eating, existing. I tried to coax her to seek professional help because I though that with counselling and associating with others who have been through the loss of a child she would realize that she was not alone, that others have been hurt and are hurting. There is some consolation in shared misery. But she refused and struggled on in her own path.

She died recently, and although the death certificate didn't state it, a major contributing factor was her broken heart. She may have felt, as many have felt, that she was losing her mind in grief, but she was really losing her heart.

Many will say these reactions are all normal and, as long as they don't go on for years, they too shall pass. In some cases, only professional help and counselling will be able to sort it all out effectively.

I think that it is very important to grieve and not to be controlled by what others may think is appropriate. In this fast paced society we seem to feel that a man or woman returning to work should be able to do so within a certain time frame. We no longer wear black arm bands to tell the world that a loved one has died. There are tell-tale signs though and society should pay attention to them. When I came back to work, my first day on the radio was very difficult. I thought I was coping well and reading from a script just as I had read before Teddy's death. I finished my appearance on the show and went back to the office from the studio. Shortly thereafter, the telephone rang and a woman who had called before for information, asked to speak with me. She said that she was wondering if something had happened because my voice sounded so dreadful. I said, yes, something had happened. She paused and said..."did someone die, dear?"

I said, yes my son had died. She then said she thought so because my voice sounded as though the life had been pulled from it and there was just a sound coming out. We spoke for a few moments and I was surprised that someone out there in the audience was that astute. Then again, perhaps I was simply fooling myself that I was as normal as ever.

It is important for employers to realize that the grief experienced when a child dies is so profound that it cannot even be measured. The three-day allowance for a funeral may be taken, but it will be months and years before the deepest strains of grief are even brought to the surface.

I have heard people say ... he lost his daughter six months ago and he is still upset. Unfortunately, unless one has walked along that path of grief, one cannot understand, but believe me six months is a tiny drop in a bucket when it comes to the loss of a child.

Over the years, I have spent many hours with friends and

acquaintances who have lost children in death. Their stories are always difficult and only when you expose yourself to the hurts of others, can you begin to heal a little as well ... otherwise, you do become isolated and think that you are the only person who has ever lost a child. This doesn't lessen or trivialize your own loss or grief but it does bring you to some understanding that death does happen and it happens every day.

The Christmas season following Teddy's death we were invited out to a gathering. The hostess had also invited Julia since she sensed that things must be difficult for her as well. We reluctantly went because it seemed to be a gesture that was honest and meaningful. We did enjoy ourselves, although I certainly felt very guilty that I was enjoying myself ... I felt I should be cut off from all happiness because of my grief. A woman came over to me ... I hadn't met her before. She said that she had heard about my son's death and she was very sorry.

"But," she said, "there are things worse than death. My brother was injured in an accident and he is now a vegetable. He will never practise law again, see his children, know that his wife is visiting him in the hospital, or even understand what his name is ... he would have been better off dead."

She said that she had learned so much with her brother's state and she had seen young people in the hospital who had been hurt and were in the same condition. She said that although we couldn't believe it now, someday we would see that God had been merciful and spared us all.

I was confused ... she had been pleasant and honest, and she was not being nasty, and yet the audacity that someone could say there are things worse than my son's death. Eventually, I did realize what she was saying, but for a long time her words bothered me.

I said that I felt guilty about feeling happy for a few hours. I found that every morning when I awoke for many years after his death, I would say " ... oh Teddy's dead." This was a normal morning response and I was simply identifying in my own head that once again I should realize this was not a dream, this was reality.

I was compulsive in those years after his death - I played the piano until my wrists ached. I wondered if I was trying to capture something he would have completed had he been allowed to continue with his studies. At first, I stayed away from the written word because I wasn't sure I wanted to read about death, and then once I started to read books, I devoured them. I would read all night and be bleary-eyed in the morning. Sometimes I could not recall anything that I had read. Then out of the blue on the subway or in an elevator, words would come back to me and hit me in the head and it would be a passage from a book I had read but thought I had forgotten. I sought answers everywhere I could - from other people, from music, from religion, from books. I was the seeker and I couldn't find anything that could satisfy my question ... why had he died?

I promised myself that every day for a full year I would wear

51

something that was black - even if it was a pair of gloves or socks ... somehow the world that saw me must know that I was in mourning.

I was so busy that perhaps only I noticed these strange little things I was doing. I was still working and putting out the reports and commentaries I was contracted for and I was still carrying on the duties of the house where we all sought some refuge. I wasn't really giving in to grief though because I could only do that in the spare time that was left over when everything had been completed. I was becoming emotionally exhausted. I wanted to spend more time at the cemetery because it was there that I had some contact with what had been my son.

When death did happen to my family and me, I was unprepared. I must say that today, looking back, there was one man who was absolutely wonderful. He was an older priest who was in our parish. He was from Italy and had been raised in an orphanage. It was interesting that he, who had not enjoyed the love and comfort of a family, responded so warmly to us, and each month on the 22nd day, he came to our home, spent the evening with us, prayed with us, and helped us. He came unannounced and he always laughed and smiled and played with the younger children. He really didn't have to do this, but he was a giving and loving man who cared only for the spiritual comfort of his parishioners. He was also a humble man. When we gave him a gift of money at Christmas, he thanked us and later we learned that he had bought clothes for a needy family in the parish. Although we often had a language barrier, we never had an understanding barrier.

If there is one wish for the bereaved it is to have at least one friend who can share your moments. The moments when you want to talk, those when you want silence, the times to remember your loved one, and the times to promise that you will carry on because life must go on, no matter what.

You will find solace in others as well - no matter how terrible your tragedy, there are others who have been there and have their story to tell. Sometimes, you come away and wonder how these horrible events have ever happened and how other people have managed to live through them. Sometimes, you realize that not everyone can survive these blows and traumas, and you know that no matter how horrific your life has been, others have also been hurt, have been destroyed, have suffered. Although you shudder to think of it, you also know that others will be faced with death in the future - if you can help, so much the better. If you can't, that too is all right.

And, then you realize there are many islands in that sea.

In My Thoughts

CHAPTER FIVE

TIES THAT BIND CAN ALSO CUT

The impact of a child's death can be the last straw in a marriage that has already had its problems, or it can be a strong thread that will pull things together. No one can forecast how the strength of a marriage will be tested.

In sickness and in health...in good times and in bad.

Many people have said that a mother can never get over the loss of child. Even the Bible asks, can a mother ever forget her child? And of course, the answer is no. The woman has carried that child, delivered it, nurtured it, it has become a part of her own body. The woman who has adopted a child has been through a gestation period in much the same way, although not in a physical sense. When a child dies, there is an amputation of the heart, and a part of the mother is buried with the child.

But society often gives fathers a back seat in grief. Yet their grief is so intense and the restrictions placed on them so strong - they shouldn't cry at work or show signs of weakness. They have to get out there and provide for the family; they must show they are men and be able to carry on. There is a tremendous burden placed on fathers when death hits the family.

As well, there can be guilt that the father, who is the provider and the strength behind the family, has failed. The child has died and he is to blame. Of course, this is not the case but it is a very subtle type of feeling that manages to creep into many heads. There can be a feeling of inadequacy because nothing works anymore ... everything from the moment of death has to be restructured.

One father told me that he couldn't even answer a simple question when a new acquaintance asked him how many children he had. He said that he automatically started to answer...three. Then, he thought, no, my daughter has died. Then, he thought, but she was mine and we did have her, she wasn't some figment of my imagination and she is still my daughter. The whole idea of changing the family around caused turmoil in his mind. He said that he didn't want to explain the death because he didn't know the person that well and he had learned that people often draw away when someone says that a child has died. He finally just said, "Oh, I have two children," But later he felt guilty that he hadn't recognized his dead child, that he had denied her very existence.

Women may find that they can talk a little more easily with relatives and friends about the dead child, but many men feel they must maintain a reserve and not let their emotions be seen with tears or anger or remorse.

A man I interviewed lost an adult son and he told me that it was difficult because his wife cried so much over this loss.

He said that he couldn't cry anymore and he wanted to get on with things in his own way, but felt he had to comfort her. The reactions are different in the sexes and this is one area that must be understood if there is to be adequate and meaningful communication. There are gender differences and they must be appreciated by both parties.

Many men feel that they have spent too much time in their careers and if a child has died they feel a sense of loss that they should have spent their time with the family and not in travel or on projects or working nights and weekends to get the job done. One man told me that he cursed his job for months, told his boss to go to Hell, threw away anything that reminded him of his work, which by the way had been very successful. He was blaming his career for his child's death. Coming to terms with these emotions and keeping the marriage together is difficult. In some cases there can be other problems - there may be court cases from the death, loss of income if a parent cannot resume working, financial problems, alcohol or drug addiction that worsens in times of stress, a move from the family home, changes that are tearing everyone up. Some marriages simply cannot withstand these forces, which are small volcanoes erupting on an already difficult terrain.

Counselling may be necessary for both parties so that emotions can be studied...why does he act this way? Why does she do such strange things? Children in the family may also be terribly frightened that having lost a sibling, they may now lose a parent should a separation take place.

A child's death may place an added strain on a marriage and some argue that these marriages may have failed in due course and the death was a catalyst. There is no question though that times are tough in any marriage when guilt, anger, frustration, loss of identity, and loss of self esteem are hurled around like bullets in a shooting spree. Husbands and wives do say hurtful things, do act in negative ways, and do suffer.

We often lash out at those who are closest to us and we fail to respect those we know so well.

Mothers are often placed on the pedestals of grief and people will point and say - that poor woman, she lost her child. They may simply look at the father and say that he should be trying harder to get things back to normal.

Some people will react to grief by sleeping and this can infuriate the other partner who wonders how anything will ever be accomplished. For some, sleep is a necessary escape. Some will become quite frenetic and want to turn things upside down - move to another house away from memories, throw out things that belonged to the child, get rid of the dog, buy a dog, sell the cottage because there are so many memories there, even change eating patterns or leisure activities. A war can rage and the two countries, of husband and wife can destroy themselves and each other. Unfortunately, often the children become the buffer states.

When this happens, I think it is important to sit down and calmly discuss the situation. Are things so bad that the two people cannot even be in the same room? Is one partner blaming the other for the child's death because he or she was too lenient, allowed the child to do dangerous things, was not observant enough to see that there was something wrong and an illness was taking over, allowed the child to go out when dangers lurked?

A marriage may be made in Heaven, but a marriage can also go through its own Hell. It is important to know if the relationship is suffering and struggling because the seeds of discontent were there before the child died, and if the impact of death has shaken at the roots.

In some cases, there can be no growth and unfortunately, the marriage does fail. The impact of the tragedy of death is then heightened by the impact of another loss - the marriage. Sometimes, a little breathing space is needed for all parties.

The marriage may have been strained by a long, lingering death and all of the problems that translated into tiny cracks during the illness may become craters after the death of the child.

Since we all grieve differently according to our personality, outlook, or cultural background, a husband and wife can be poles apart in bereavement.

Many have said that being married was a great help because there was someone with whom to talk, discuss, and rationalize what had happened. Others have said that a wall of silence meant that grief had to be handled on one's own.

There are many feelings wrapped up in a marriage and intimacy is often difficult for some people. One woman told me that she was astonished that her husband would even consider sexual relations just a few weeks after her daughter's death. Another said that she wondered why her husband had abandoned her and why he couldn't help her and be close to her at this time.

Another told me that the thought of intimacy was upsetting since it was a reminder of the child who had been conceived in love and had now been taken away from her. She added that her husband didn't think in those terms and simply could not understand her reserve. It is never easy to return to the way things were before a death and perhaps one of the most difficult roads is that which involves our sexuality.

One man said that he felt he had suffered the loss of his wife when his child died because she was so focused on her other children, clinging to the hope that they would survive and never die as the child had died. He said she was obviously a great mother but not such a great wife.

Perhaps the realization that grief is a totally private, isolated, and a very personal process may make things more understandable. Once you realize that only you can go through that dark tunnel that appears to have no hope, no joy, no release, and you must go through it alone, you can come to terms with your spouse. Eventually, you do emerge and you do see that there is some light, there may be some joy, and there will be a release from the stranglehold of death in its initial throes. It may be that you can also see that your spouse has also been traveling through that tunnel and has had to come to terms with feelings that may never have even been considered before death hit.

Again, it is important to try to see the other point of view without being blinded by your own devastation. It may be that the marriage cannot go on and for all concerned the tunnels will be separate and have different endings.

'Till death do us part.

In My Thoughts

CHAPTER SIX

HEAL THYSELF ...

*M*y head was exploding, my heart was thumping, my body was shaking, I couldn't focus my eyes properly, I was sure that a building was going to come down on top of me. For a moment, I thought I was in the middle of a movie set and expected that apes would descend upon me from another planet. I staggered, and then I was draped over a newspaper box on the street. The world was spinning around me. No one bothered to ask if I needed help. Somehow, I managed to return back to the studio where I worked, and I phoned my husband. As I sat in the foyer of the building, a co-worker rushed by, and without missing a beat said ...

" Hi, how are you," and walked away.

I thought, I guess I must be fine!

If you don't see it, it can't be there ...

When I suffered this strange reaction, it was in the month of October, just a few days before the anniversary of my son's death. I thought that since four years had passed I was fine - physically, emotionally, mentally. After all, if anything was going to happen, it would have happened sooner.

I went to the doctor later that day. My hands were icy cold although it was a warm day in the autumn. The doctor said that my blood pressure was quite low and perhaps I should have some tests. Calls were made and in the days to follow I was given glucose tolerance tests, tests to measure brain waves (I wondered what they found?) and a number of other tests. The results were mixed. I was told by one specialist that it could be one of five conditions ranging from a tumour to infection. I asked each doctor if this type of condition with vertigo and pain in the head could be related to stress or grief. I was given a strange look every time I asked. The doctors didn't seem too interested in the fact that for the past four years I had been busy with keeping things going - a family, a house, a cottage, a job. As well, we had lost other family members - since my son's death, my father-in-law and a younger brother-in-law had died. Perhaps I hadn't spent enough time trying to come to terms with my losses. Again, there were the looks that said it all. No, they didn't think that after so many years, when everything seemed so right and there were no addictions or strange types of behaviour, I could be in grief and be suffering any grief-related reactions.

I started to wonder. A friend who had lost a son in an accident often said to me that he had not wanted to see his son's body after the accident. He had been shattered by the whole idea of his son's death and he simply wanted to remember him as he had been. A few years later, this man had an operation on his eyes. He did wonder if his eye problems were remotely related to the importance he had placed on not wanting to look at his son.

It is difficult to know if people do develop illnesses that are related to their unresolved grief.

I do know that many physicians are not comfortable talking about death and about grieving. They may be uncomfortable because they are unsure of their own emotions ... perhaps they see too much of death and they are not sure how they should convey their feelings to a patient.

I think that it is very important for a bereaved parent or sibling or grandparent to have a doctor who will take the time to answer questions. Many doctors will offer medication to help with sleeping, anxiety, or stress. This may not always be the answer. Sometimes, a quiet moment or two just listening will work miracles. A doctor I was fortunate enough to meet soon after my son's death was also a bereaved parent and he said that there were times when he would start to cry while he had patients in his office. I asked him what he did when this happened and he said he cried and told the patient that he had lost a child and if he couldn't cry for his own child, for whom could he cry? I am sure that doctor always listened when a patient in grief came to his office.

While the outward signs of grief - crying, agonizing over the death, changes in mood, fatigue and depression, may last for a long time, it is important to try to find out if there is anything underlying that may be causing other problems. Certainly the bereaved are vulnerable, and it is important to keep health in check. Some people will throw all caution to the wind and indulge in food, alcohol and drugs at this time.

Any behaviour that is dangerous must be curbed. It is the subtle conditions, though, that are often overlooked and can be most harmful...the things we don't always see as we chat with friends and neighbours. I am thinking of the pains in the head, stomach, the eating disorders, the patterns that spell illness.

I have said that society today wants to have a timetable for everything, but grief has its own yardstick. One person may appear to be fine after a year, another may take two, three, even five years to start to come back. The return to some semblance of a normal life is important, not only for the bereaved but for their families.

Many people have told me that they noted a turning point in their lives when suddenly a veil seemed to lift from them. Sometimes, this was traumatic and was the result of something else happening to them that shook them out of their own grieving. For others, it was a natural evolution that time provided.

I remember one woman whose son had died in the early spring. She was distraught and every time I saw her I thought how much she resembled me when I was in the same time frame of grief. Her eyes were dull and lifeless, she no longer spoke with a sparkle as she had in previous times, she walked with her shoulders hunched over, and she looked several years older than she was. She hesitated now before she spoke. Before her son's death she had always laughed and talked in an animated and happy way, throwing her hands around in the conversation to emphasize each word.

70

Whenever we met, I put my arm around her shoulder, and together we cried.

One day about a year after her son's death and in the spring, she saw me and she smiled and said that she knew for certain that everything would be fine. She had looked out of her window and had seen the flowers poking their heads up in her garden.

She said that when her son died, she hadn't noticed the flowers all of that summer and she truly felt they would never come to life again. Suddenly, with the passage of time, she saw new life in her garden and she related that to her own feelings. She had been working through her grief no doubt and was coming to some terms with her loss.

There are also little things which are difficult to explain to others who have never been through the death of a child. There is so much searching that goes on it is almost impossible to stop looking at every moment for a sign that the child's spirit is somehow with you. You look into a crowd and you are sure he is there walking along. You hear someone who laughs as he laughed and you wonder if that is really him. You dream about strange and sometimes frightening situations. I recall that soon after his death I was dreaming that Teddy was standing beside my bed. He held his hand to his head and said that everything was fine and I shouldn't worry. I asked if his head was hurting. He said he was fine.

But I felt that he was in pain.

When I awoke I was certain he had been in that room. My logical side kept saying, don't be so silly, but my emotional side kept saying ... he was here, I know he was. I was torn that morning as I thought about the strangest dream I had ever had. I wondered if I was really losing it and how my children would cope if their mother was suffering a breakdown. Then, I rationalized that Teddy's death was only a short 10 days ago and I was probably still in shock. That morning, the coroner phoned and told me that he had the death certificate and the report.

I asked about Teddy's injuries and the cause of death. I asked if Teddy had injured his head. The coroner said yes, and his ear was badly burned.

His ear was badly burned ... I had seen him holding his head and covering his ear. I hadn't seen him at the hospital because I couldn't bear to look. I had never seen him in the coffin because it had been closed. At that point, I was even more convinced that he had indeed been at my bedside.

I didn't say anything to anyone. After all, I had a reputation as an investigative reporter ... I didn't believe anything anyone told me. I always had to find out for myself. My kids had dubbed my the "Cynic" and "Doubting Thomasina." How could I ever say that I knew in a dream something which I later learned to be true?

My turning point came much later and it wasn't anything that was earth shattering or spectacular. Most mornings I would wake up and my first thoughts were Teddy - he was not here, I would think, and the whole scenario would run through my head. I would recall details of the funeral, think about people who had angered me, offended me, think about how I would have changed everything from the funeral to the cemetery. I could only focus on death. Then, one day, I awoke and I was actually laughing. I must have been dreaming and my thoughts were bright, fresh, and funny. I was laughing at something that must have been hilarious although I couldn't for the life of me think of what it was. All day, I was in a good mood.

Then, at night, I realized that I hadn't thought about Teddy all day.

I felt terribly guilty and upset and felt that I was being disloyal to his memory. This must have been well over a year after his death, perhaps closer to two years. I realized that I could laugh and enjoy my children, my husband, my relatives, and my work once again if I tried.

I didn't have to abandon his memory. From that day on for whatever reason, I began to heal.

Another woman told me recently that she found solace in the sea after her daughter's death. She had been living a life of total unhappiness for about 18 months following the girl's death. Then, one day, she sat on a beach and just watched the waves beat against the shore and she felt that she was spiritually connected to her daughter and that everything was fine.

Although these moments may beckon a new era in life, there are also the times when regression sets in, and again those overwhelming feelings of despair take over. Every little bit of success will bring you closer to recovery, and it is important to be thankful and to recognize the healing as it comes.

Doctors cannot heal everything that happens - they can't always bring a patient back to health and they can't always bring the bereaved back to health. They can, however, recognize that the death of a child is so brutal that the whole body of the grief-stricken can be affected. I would hope that more and more doctors will recognize that patients do need special care in these times, and I do know that those doctors who have experienced tragedies in their own lives are often the most successful at helping others.

Doctors can look for signs, though, that indicate that grief is very much at work. A patient who has lost a child may present with a variety of physical problems - a feeling that a heart attack is imminent, shortness of breath, a feeling of pressure in the chest, dry mouth, anxiety bordering on panic, lack of energy, fatigue, depression, confusion, sleep disturbances, withdrawal from society, nightmares, appetite changes such as compulsive eating or abstaining from food, forgetfulness. The list could go on forever. Sometimes, the best medicine is to allow the parent or sibling to just talk about all of the things that are racing through the mind. Giving permission to the bereaved to yell, be angry, and express the hurt that has hit the heart can be beneficial.

Explaining that extreme behaviour changes are normal in a state of grief can often lessen the concerns the person may be experiencing.

There are some little things that may stick with the person for years - for instance I find that whenever I lose something - and it can be something quite inconsequential, I become very upset. I will root through boxes of files, look through cupboards, search the garage, and then I ask myself why I am doing this. At that point, I realize once again, that I am really upset that I lost a child and I want to prevent my losing anything else. Once I come to terms with this I am fine. However, it still happens and it has become a quirk in my personality. Perhaps, when I can sit back and say, okay, I lost a book or I have misplaced a file, I will be healthier. But until then, I have to live with myself and simply say that this is a reminder that I have lost something so important in my life I have to protect everything I own.

There can be dreadful flashbacks ... times we have to face in our lives, but times that are devastating. One mother told me that she had to visit her mother in the Intensive Care Unit and she relived her child's last moments. A father mentioned that every time he saw a baby's crib, he broke down and cried.

Although circumstances may be different, just being in certain places can bring back memories too painful to even discuss. For any parent who had to spend time in a court room listening to testimony surrounding a child's death, the very thought of returning to that environment can produce trauma for days and weeks.

This is one area that I think we must touch on - people would say to me that the bereaved often seek revenge if the child has died in an accident, as the result of a murder, or through negligence. This may be true in some instances. Yet deep down we know that nothing will return that child to us. We also know that if we can prevent such a death from ever occurring again, we will want to do that and we will do that, and that is not revenge, it is love and concern for others.

In healing ourselves it is important that we take the time to stop and think about the effects that death can have on every aspect of our being. It may be a good idea to take a long quiet walk when you think you need it and forget your work. It may be fine to sit down and enjoy a special treat the way you once did with your child. It may be a good idea to listen to music for a day and forget the laundry and the cleaning and the cooking. It may be worthwhile to spend some time on yourself so that when you look in the mirror you see the old self that was there before the child died ... the face that your child could remember. It may be that on a rainy afternoon curling up with a good book can work wonders in bringing you back to life. It may be that digging up the garden with such force that you let out your own pent up emotions can be healthy. And, it may be that crying for your child is one of the best ways to heal yourself.

For many people, simply sitting down and writing a poem or reconstructing the events that led up to the death will be therapeutic. For many, writing a letter to the child and expressing your innermost feelings and apologizing for things in the past, can be a cleansing experience.

Physical health is, of course, important in your recovery; but so are mental and emotional health and this is important as you deal with your other children.

Many parents are caught in trying to protect their surviving children with a shield that may stifle them.

There is such fear when a child dies that many parents are terrified to allow their other children to do anything. And healing is needed here as well. I kept thinking that I really didn't want to see the younger children reach the age of 16 because something might happen to them as it had to their brother. This was totally irrational and without any common sense, yet I felt this way. As each child passed that landmark birthday, I sighed a prayer of relief that we had been spared.

Many parents do not want to see their surviving children play football, drive a car, ride a bike, engage in sports that could be dangerous. They have such fear that once again they will lose a child. This is a dangerous situation for them as the other children may grow up resenting the dead child and being angry at the parents. Few children are able to fully understand why their parents feel this way and they can become very angry about the treatment they feel they are receiving unnecessarily.

At some point, parents and children must sit down together and work these feelings out. No one can dictate what actions are right or wrong, but this can be a stumbling block for years and with the death of a child in a family there are enough problems without introducing more.

I said earlier that when my sister died, I think her cause of death was partially a broken heart. You can't see a broken heart and it has been a term used in poetry and literature for years. Because we don't see it, it can still be there. Sometimes those things we don't see are far more painful and damaging than those which show up on an x-ray or through a battery of tests.

If you wait until you can see it ... it may be too late.

In My Thoughts

CHAPTER SEVEN

CUSTOMS OF MOURNING

We all celebrate in different ways. When we marry, we wear our own traditional clothes. When we gather together, we eat our own favourite foods. When we bury our dead and mourn, we have our own ways, and there is never a right way or a wrong way, there is only our own way.

> *Some say that tears are a sign of weakness,*
> *Some say that tears are a sign of truth.*

There are many faces in grief and each is so special. I found that my reactions were quite different from those of my husband. My family background is Canadian with Irish and Scottish parents; my husband's is Polish.

I remembered the death of one of my father's uncles when I was a young child. I remember that my father and my brother were invited to go to the farm and sit with the body all night because the custom then was to keep the deceased at home rather than in a funeral home.

I heard stories about Irish wakes and how they were not solemn, but rather a time of celebration. The families and friends would come with food, drink, and wishes that the life had been good and the next life would be even better. There was a strong belief in Heaven and the rewards that come from a long and worthy life. Death was not to be feared because it was a natural and normal passage into the next world. In fact, someone said that death was no more than life changing addresses.

On the Scottish side of the family I had heard stories about great Uncle Peter and his death at his farm. I wondered about the custom of putting coins on his eyelids. I was told that a funeral must be dignified - and a little less boisterous than the Irish side of the family.

My husband's reactions to Teddy's death were solemn, angry, unbelieving. He was more open in his grief and his feelings, while I tried to keep my emotions held in by a tight rein.

In our case, the funeral was difficult and a part of me didn't want to be there. But, another part would not let go and I wondered if perhaps we could hold on to the coffin and Teddy's remains for a few days more and if that might act as a security blanket for all of us. The funeral service was in a church and Mass was celebrated by the priests of the parish. The music was all of his favourites - from *Swan Lake* and the *Song of Joy* I wondered why we had ever chosen that since this was certainly not a time of joy. It had been his favourite however, so we asked for it. As his coffin was wheeled from the church, his friends quietly sang "We Shall Overcome" and I wondered if we would ever overcome the mountain of sorrow hanging over us all. The custom of bringing the deceased to church for a last time was important to us and it did serve to allow his friends and our family to be together.

Not all families will want this; and for some people, a service with very little music or words is important - there can be healing in quiet.

A few years ago, a neighbour lost a baby to crib death. I was terribly upset and once again wondered how an innocent child who was so beautiful and so perfect could have died. The family is Chinese and the symbols they gave to us at the funeral home were very moving - an envelope with a coin and a candy. An aunt explained that these were to bring happiness back and we should eat the candy and spend the coin. I thought about it and prayed that the baby would have a sweet passing. I prayed also for the comfort and peace of the parents.

There are many customs which are important for each nationality, religion, and group, and each has immeasurable value.

Over the years, I have come to realize that no matter how we say farewell to our children, the faces of grief are always the same. The customs may be different, but the look is always the same. It is a look that only those who have been there can recognize in another. There is a fraternity out there and although no one wears buttons or has a secret handshake, we do recognize little things that make us one.

We also have customs in remembering our children and sometimes these evolve over the years in little ways. We always go to the cemetery on the anniversary of his death and bring flowers. We remembered him for the first few years with a scholarship for an outstanding young person in the drum corps. Other families have instituted scholarships in memory of their children or have provided worthwhile monuments in gifts to others and to projects, and in giving to charity in memory of the child.

Many people can only wear dark colours. Many groups only wear black after the death of a family member and some wear white ...I must say that I did follow my own tradition and wore something black for about a year. It made me feel as though I was showing the world I was in mourning, although I am sure that anyone seeing my face and my expression didn't have to look at the colour of my clothes to know that something was very wrong.

Whether we are surrounded by flowers at the funeral home or have none, whether we sing or are silent, whether we fall on our knees over the grave or stand by as the body is cremated, it is all the right way since we have chosen it.

If anything, I have learned that every custom has its place and each must be respected.

I learned that tears are a sign of love for our dead children.

In My Thoughts

CHAPTER EIGHT

WHY HAVE YOU FORSAKEN ME?

*B*ecause the death of a child is so unnatural, many people feel they must have done something wrong - they were evil in another time, they are being punished for their wrong doings, they didn't appreciate what they had and so they had to lose it. The rational side of thinking is lost for a time and grief becomes 'crazy' and wild. For some, turning to religion will provide answers, for others turning away from religion is a necessary step.

Where were You when I needed You most?

Over the years, I have spoken with dozens of people who have lost their children in death. Many have complained that they sought help from their religious leaders, but found absolutely no solace, no understanding, no sense of peace, and they had to look to themselves for answers, or turn away entirely. Many do not want their names mentioned and we will simply refer to them anonymously.

For some people, the role the clergy played was most valuable in their recovery and they point to the importance of having a strong spiritual link with a pastor or a rabbi. For others, a sense of inner peace came from reading, listening to music, walking through nature, watching the birds, or just looking at the sea.

Here are their stories:

"When my child died, I found I could not find anything which answered my questions - all the why's, the reasons for this tragedy. One priest simply said ... "Have faith." I wanted to punch him ... have faith, damn it! I always had faith. I had faith my child would grow up and outlive me. I had faith I would see him graduate from university. I had faith in everything I ever did. I didn't know, though, that he would die and I would be left without any answers. And, I thought for some reason that a man of the cloth could have explained something to me in a better way than with two useless words. Now, I don't go to church, and I don't discuss religion."

"My husband and I were worlds apart. He has never been one to go to church and over the years I guess I didn't bother either. But when my son died, I felt his presence around me and I knew that the actual church building was not necessary, but the spiritual connection was there between us. I have often dreamed about him and I know that God is caring for him whether I attend church or not."

"When I knew my child was dead, I wanted to rip God's head right off ... I stood in the emergency room and tore a tissue to shreds and cursed. I guess that I have been angry for so long, I can't return now."

"I have long conversations with God - I yell at Him and tell Him that I think this has been a dirty trick He has played on us all. But, I'm not really so angry that I stay away from church or stop believing. I just think that when I communicate in my way I can yell and holler at what I perceive God to be and then I do feel better."

"When my son died I felt a calm flood over me. I know there were other emotions, but for whatever reason there was this calm and I somehow felt he was fine and God was caring for him."

"I have had recurring dreams that my children are drowning and I can't get to them on time."

"When I asked for a memorial Mass, the priest said he would fit it in. I said I wanted it on the anniversary of my child's death. He simply smiled and said that he would try. I told him that this was important to me as a parent, but he really didn't understand what I was trying to say. I didn't want something 'fitted in' and I was very angry. I eventually went to another church."

"My wife will not go near the synagogue or participate in any religious holidays anymore. She simply says that there cannot be a God who would allow these things to happen. I feel sorry for her in this regard, because I think it must be difficult."

"I went to church every chance I got ... I wondered to myself if I were able to spend more time in worship, would I be protecting myself. And, I also found that I was really getting something out of being in that quiet sanctuary where I felt that I was linked to something much greater and bigger than myself or my grief. Religion helped me and it still does."

"My grandmother told me that when her first child died, she cried night and day. When her second child died, she didn't cry at all. She said that God was going to look after things. But, I wonder if she was really just all cried out and she couldn't cope or she was just afraid that a third child might die as well. It was wartime and who knows what happens in those cases."

"I heard that in death, the slate is wiped clean. I never appreciated what that meant. But, my uncle would tell me that and wipe tears from his eyes. He said that a learned rabbi had given him that information. For whatever reason, I felt a little better after hearing it. My child had a difficult death."

"My thoughts were to help the rest of the world. I could never do anything for my child so I was going to set out and follow my religious convictions and help others. It took me to new places and new realizations that we are all linked somehow whether through God or some other strength, and we had better put ourselves to good works while we can."

"I kept thinking about that baby I lost before it was born and I wondered why this had happened. No one could appreciate that this was a loss and just because I hadn't held the child or seen it, that child was still mine and had died before it had lived. I pray every day to God to protect this angel and to help me."

"Every year on the anniversary of my child's death, I spend the day away from work. I go to church - any church as long as it is open. I go to the cemetery, and then I have a great lunch, see a movie, and enjoy myself...I am happy that God gave me my child and we had time together. I can't spend any more time in yelling at religion or myself."

"I think that men and women who are involved in religion should learn a little more about life - what to say to someone who is bitter, hurt, and angry. We can't always be nice guys and if the ministers, priests, and rabbis and the other religious clergy can't get it, then we don't need them."

"The only solace I found was in my faith - I prayed, prayed, prayed, and through that prayer I was able to get through the worst time of my life. I think that everyone needs religion, no matter what that religion is, because strong faith heals the wounded."

"I eventually did get over my daughter's death - it was difficult and it took about 15 years, but today I appreciate everything I have in my life and I appreciate the years I had with her. I can't pinpoint when it happened, but it was a strange and warm feeling that I could survive and be happy for her and for me."

"I went through a terrible time in my life - I lost a child, my husband left, but I persevered and I did feel better when I had a connection with my church because it seemed to be the only stable influence in my life. For whatever reason, it made a difference."

"I was bitter for many years, but now I cherish everything I have. I still cry at the mention of her name, but I also know that I must love my family more and more. Something positive finally came from her death...but if things could be different I would trade everything I have to have her again."

"We were new to Canada and our ways were different. I was shy about my customs, and now I feel guilty because I should have followed my own feelings when my son died. I feel that I denied myself and him and now I have to make up for it."

"I learned we have to be careful what we pray for ... my child was suffering so much with cancer that I couldn't face it. I prayed that God would take her. But when she died, I felt guilty, and now I can only pray she is at peace."

"Now I understand, we are in the same boat now."

The last quote came from a friend whose son died about five years after my son in a similar accident. When she came to my door one afternoon she simply said "we are in the same boat now."

I couldn't comprehend what she was talking about but I knew from her eyes and her speech something was wrong. Then, she told me about her son. And I knew that she did understand.

Another friend came to me in recent years and said that she had been so sure of herself and her faith when Teddy died that she felt she had to lecture me. She told me that things were fine because he was in Heaven. When one of her nieces died, she said she had to apologize because suddenly all of those words she had spewed forth at me were really senseless and so much idle talk. She said that she had spoken as if she really knew something when she couldn't have possibly been able to know.

I have found that some of the most religious and fervent people say some of the silliest things when they are faced with death. They may feel that everything in life is simply pre-destined and we have to accept what happens. We often see, though, that they have never been through these situations.

I think that it is important to realize that it doesn't matter how old a parent may be when death strikes the child, the feelings are as intense for an old person as they are for a young parent. People must realize that the older bereaved parent must be helped through those times and given special considerations as well as love and care.

After Teddy died, many people came to me and said, "It is God's will."

Maybe it was, I don't know. At the initial period of grief, I was quite angry when I heard those words. I don't really think that God wills any child to die in an accident, in illness, in murder, in suicide, in any way. I think that things happen and the child dies. A car drives in the wrong lane and kills the child. Cancer strikes and the child dies. A murderer preys on a victim and kills her. And so on it goes...death happens and death hurts. When death is fresh in the head and the heart, it may be best to say less rather than more, and simply give the family support and not empty words and patronizing philosophy.

I found that I had different needs in different stages of mourning. Initially, I couldn't concentrate enough to read even the daily paper. I didn't want to know what was happening in the world because it didn't really mean anything to me. I shunned television because everything reminded me of violence and death from the late news to the mystery stories. I was angered by television crews that wanted to focus on the guts of death and suffering. In fact, I remember phoning one station and lodging a complaint and asking why they had to run pictures of the morgue - was it really necessary for the story content?

In time and in another stage of my grief, I found I needed to read as much as I could so that I could come to an understanding of what death was all about. Sometimes, I wanted only to hear music...requiems, chants, and string quartets.

Soon after Teddy's death, I may have learned something, although at the time I was unsure. I was hanging laundry in the yard and it was a cold November day. I was preoccupied with grief and was doing everything in robot style. As I hung the clothes, a butterfly settled on the clothes line. This seemed out of place - it wasn't a warm summer day, it was a cold, grey, November day, and yet a butterfly was on the clothesline. I had read about the butterfly in many pieces of literature over the years, and a friend had explained that he believed the butterfly symbol was important in grief. Even that encounter had been interesting. He was an announcer at the CBC and when he heard about Teddy's death, he invited me for coffee in the old cafeteria on Jarvis Street. We went through the line for our drinks and he suggested we have something to eat since we had been on air and had missed lunch. When we got to the cashier, he looked embarrassed and said..."damn, I forget my money...will you buy me lunch?" We laughed and talked about the Irish treat - we both ate and I paid!

He then talked about the importance of looking for little signs that Teddy was fine and he said that he really did believe in the butterfly as the symbol of the psyche. He added, "With this weather, you'll have to wait until spring." We laughed and I went home.

It was the next day that the butterfly came to my clothesline. I couldn't help remembering his words, and from then on I seemed to see a lot of butterflies everywhere.

Interestingly , I have recently renewed acquaintances with a godson, Richard, who was born in the same year as my son. When we met for lunch a few years ago, one of the first topics of conversation was his interest in butterflies... we spent most of our visit talking about them. Recently, we

95

enjoyed another lunch and he brought me a necklace with a hand carved wooden butterfly. Perhaps, this really is the butterfly effect.

So, while I believe that religion helped me through the rough spots, I also believe that there is a spiritual connection that binds us with our children.

I do believe in the power of prayer for me. I also believe in meditation because it can take you away from the busy world and allow you time to quietly work out your feelings. I also think that this respite can allow you to come back with a fresher outlook and a renewed spirit.

I believe in the quiet times when you can reach into your memories, think about your own soul, and deep down, know that everything is fine.

I was with you, but you didn't see Me.

In My Thoughts

CHAPTER NINE

TURN TO JOY

$\mathcal{L}$ife can never be the same - everyday you notice something that is now different. You look at the clock and it is time for your child to be returning from school, play, work, or a holiday, but he doesn't come in the door.

You set the table and there is an empty spot. You look in his room and nothing has been moved around - the clothes are hung neatly now, there are no candy wrappers on the floor, no running shoes that should have been thrown out long ago, no records stacked on the bed, no reason for you to yell at him and tell him to clean up his act. You shop for gifts but the birthday is not going to come and when you plan an anniversary party you have second thoughts because he was going to be the master of ceremonies but, he won't be there.

An explosion ripped him from our lives ...

Soon after Teddy died, we went as a family to a restaurant to celebrate my birthday. I really didn't want to go, but the children said it was going to be a big surprise and so I played along. My husband was trying to do something that would ease our grief. I acted with surprise and we were enjoying a pleasant meal. The younger children indicated that they had a special secret and when the waiter came with a large

99

birthday cake, they pointed to it and said it was their gift. I was doing well and enjoying these moments. Then, the waiter brought the plates and said ..." Now, we have seven slices, is that right?"

Oh yes, I thought, it is right...there were only six of us, but the waiter thought there were seven. I was elated in one way that Teddy's presence was somehow there but sad in another that he wasn't there physically.

Whether it was coincidence or whether the waiter just couldn't count it doesn't matter...it was a strange and somehow wonderful moment that indicated to me that Teddy was nearby in some form.

I can't explain things that happen like that, but they do happen. Many will say it is only coincidence and you shouldn't even think about it, since it means nothing. Usually the people who say those things have never been through the death of a child.

All religious holidays are terrible times when your child is not with you - how will you ever celebrate again? If you have other children you must allow them their time to enjoy the season. This is not easy, but it is important because every child is cherished and of great value in your life and you cannot deny them because another child has died.

Family gatherings are difficult. Six years after Teddy's death our daughter was married. Having received the photos back from the photographer we were looking at a family shot. One of her friends pointed to a space and said that that would have been where Teddy would have been standing. She was right of course and the photographer would not have known there had ever been another member of the family, and yet he had posed us this way with an empty space in the portrait.

On Christmas Eve, in the Polish tradition, we always set an extra place at the table. This has been done through the years to welcome a stranger who may come by. The setting has all of the cutlery, a piece of unleavened bread, and a napkin. That first year it was heart-wrenching to set that place. Each year that followed and each year to come there are tears on the table.

Reaching out though, can help - the year that our neighbour's baby died, we wondered about them on Christmas Eve. My daughter went over with a gift for their other child and our friend asked if she could bring her little boy over to see the tree. We invited this family for dinner and set up another table. The one place setting that year expanded to include three more and in many ways that was one of the nicest Christmas Eve dinners we have had.

The bereaved can become more sensitive to the needs of others, and that has to be one of the most positive things that comes from tragedy. You can spot someone who needs a word or two ... you can sense what others are going through ... you can reach out and try to get them over that hurdle of sorrow.

Your happiness may not be the knee-slapping and riotous

type, but it can be deep and serene and wonderful. It can be an expansion of yourself and have a depth of meaning that will touch your very soul.

You will have to re-educate yourself in almost everything you do as you progress. Parts of you may never ever mend or heal and you must come to terms with that, as well. Your own relationship with your children is important. Before Teddy's death, we all had such ambitions - university, awards, we would be the best on the block, never mind the whole country. Suddenly, all of that was so futile and puerile. Death had knocked down our dreams.

Today, I think with different priorities ... I see the children to be as fine as they are ... they have all worked hard, have determined their ambitions, and have, I think, been touching and caring in their own ways.

We are not unique, over and over again, you hear bereaved families say that they are surprised how tender and kind their own children are and how they can help others in the same boat of grief.

There are many positive elements that can evolve from this most negative of all happenings - the death of a child.

It is important to focus on these things and have them lift your heart and your spirits.

There will also be joy in little things in life. I said that priorities do change, and those things that were so important before death may now have no meaning or very little at most.

There can be happiness in seeing birds, flowers, hearing music, reading a book. There can be eruptions of mood as well, when you read about a senseless death.

Sometimes the emotions are just beneath the surface, and although you may feel they are no longer with you, they may indeed be very present.

The old scars are there and I guess it will take forever to learn to live with them.

I thought that at the ten year mark, I was strong and would be able to work as a volunteer in a palliative care unit in a local hospital. When I began training for this work, I found I had vertigo, headaches, and anxiety. Obviously, I wasn't ready, and I may never be ready to face this type of work. Perhaps, the scars are just too deep.

One of my greatest fears was the future ... how could I ever live another 20 years and be able to remember everything I needed to remember. I said earlier we had a portrait painted and this hangs in the dining room. I do remember what I need to remember and although it is almost 20 years now, that fear has never materialized.

Music brings back good memories, although at one time I couldn't bear to hear the songs he loved. In his knapsack there was a copy of the *Homecoming* and even today when I hear that I always stop and listen. It was significant I think that music would have been a favourite...was it a message that his would be a different homecoming?

And, God cradled him in His arms.

In My Thoughts

CHAPTER TEN

LOSSES

*T*he loss of a child is the loss of your future as well as the child's and it is also the loss of the present. Someone wrote that it was the period coming before the end of the sentence and everything was suddenly unfinished business from that point on. You could never have a chance to say once again - "You know I really love you" and you can never hear these words in return. You have only memories to sustain you and some of them can be difficult and negative. If you could only sit down and talk things over and fix the wrong parts in your relationship. However, you can't and you have to live with that side of your grief forever.

Of all the saddest words, of mouth and pen,
the saddest of these...

There can be good grief that is positive and healing, and it can come at different times for different people. It can also be interpreted differently. I think that what I have learned in these past 19 years is that you must march to your own drummer and not be too concerned with what society may establish as a 'good healing time.'

Your heart will tell you when the healing is taking place, not someone's textbook.

The clock will tick according to your own pendulum and this is important.

I know that there are things that I do, sometimes without even thinking, that indicate that grief is still a very significant part of my being. I often pick flowers from the garden and arrange them in vases. One day, a relative asked why I always chose five of one variety for the arrangements. I had been doing this since 1975 - often choosing four of the same colour and one of a different shade. Perhaps, in my subconscious, I was making a statement that these are the symbols of the children - four are the same, one is different. I also did this with pictures I made for the cottage - I had purchased five appliqués which I framed. It was only when they were on the wall that one of the children said - " Oh, I see the one with the lighter background must be Teddy."

Perhaps we always look for and incorporate symbolism into our daily lives and this in itself may be part of the healing.

I don't know if I will ever arrange the flowers differently. Perhaps this is one of the lingering signs within myself that I am acknowledging something that is different.

I think that you have to work at grief, so that in time, it becomes good grief. I was picking the weeds from the patio one afternoon and I thought that I would never finish - the more I uprooted, the more I saw. From a distance, the patio looked messy. Up close, it was showing some positive signs with a few cleared patches. Then, once I had eliminated most of the weeds, it looked great from a distance; but up close, there were still traces of dandelions.

I wondered if this was a game of perception - what we want to see, what we don't want to see. Perhaps that is really what happens as we wander through our grieving.

You can tackle weeds with heavy duty weed killers, but you may also hurt the good flowers or yourself. You can tug away at them and hope that in getting rid of the weeds, you have a cleaner and clearer picture. You can let them grow and pull them away one at a time. You can simply cover them and not look at them and not allow anyone else to look at them. The weeds will still be there; and at some point, they may have to be considered. You can also build around them with flowers that will eat out the weeds and you can find new designs so that the patio can once again be attractive and healthy. In many ways, working through your grief can be very much like working through the weeds. It is your own choice.

And really this is what grief is - choices. You must give yourself permission to grieve in your own way and you must allow others their way, as well.

At some point, you must also give yourself permission to stop grieving.

You can control your emotions quite often when you work and socialize, but if there is deep-seated anxiety, you can't always control your nightmares. This can be an indication of your own feelings about your journey.

I found that for many years following my son's death, I no longer experienced a sense of fear for myself - you know the type that grips you in the pit of your stomach. It seemed that nothing could frighten me, and perhaps that too was an indication that grief was so overpowering that I was unaware of anything that could possibly hit me again.

Many parents will say they mark their lives according to what came before the death of their child and that which came after. Over and over again, you hear them say - "Oh, we bought the house after Karen's death" or "Yes, we went to Disney the year before Matthew died."

The child's death becomes the dividing line of existence.

Many people also see the year of the child's death as a marker in their own lives. Although the birth certificate may say 56, that person may feel that life ended at 35 when the child died.

Many parents feel they have failed as a parent because the child has died, and the parent is ultimately responsible for the child forever. This can happen with parents who are elderly and still feel responsible for children who are well into adulthood.

When a child dies, there are feelings of inadequacy that everything is failure because the child has died. This can have an effect on careers, families, any growth in the parent.

There can be a feeling that you will never be in step again with the rest of the world and you really may not even want to be a part of the world as you know it since it has been so cruel.

Your own emotions can be a difficult partner to live with for the rest of your life. But, not an impossible partner. Somehow, you must learn to like yourself again, to forgive yourself if you feel guilty, to know that you have permission to cry, laugh, enjoy.

One cannot help thinking how the child would react to any situation ... how she would look as her friends now graduate from high school, how he would respond to his nieces and nephews. Knowing that the child was a gift is often a good way of coping with these feelings. There will always be that space in your life, but it can be filled with happy memories.

What might have been ...

In My Thoughts

CODA

RECOVERY

We all recover differently from physical illnesses and accidents, and much will depend on our own struggles, our immune system, our genes, our will. This can also be the case in the recovery from the death of a child.

To everything there is a season...

Some will argue that you can never recover from the death of a child, that you simply learn to cope, and you come to terms with your loss. I think this is true; but I also think that just as we recover from surgery and disease and accidents, we do experience a kind of recovery. It will not be a return to the life we knew or the feelings we experienced before the child's death because we have very deep emotional scar tissue. We can find ourselves in a new place as the healing takes over.

You may wonder why I called this chapter Coda. As a student, I was always intrigued with the order of composition in music. I always enjoyed the Coda because it brought to conclusion the mystery, the joy, the sadness, the intensity of a symphony. I would like to look back and see Teddy's life as a symphony - a time that embraced all of the emotions and joys we shared. May this Coda honour his symphony of life.

The 'firsts' are the most difficult - the first anniversary of the death, the first birthday following the death, the first Christmas, the first Chanukah, all of the firsts that hit you when you realize that the child will not be there.

The days leading up to these dates can be horrific and many people have told me that they simply wanted the calendar to go away because they couldn't face the trauma of reliving what had happened. Many also said that they were amazed because once the date arrived, they found it was not as bad as they had anticipated.

Often, we prepare ourselves for the worst, and then we find it isn't quite as bad as we thought it would be. Because that "first" date is often terrible, this doesn't automatically mean that the second anniversary will be any easier, often, we are subjected to different stresses and pressures which can make subsequent anniversaries as difficult.

The changing seasons can be very trying for the first few years - the death of summer as the leaves fall and the flowers die, the chill of winter with snow and ice, the spring that never really brings any warmth, just rain and dull weather, and the summer that seems stifling with humidity and heat.

With time, the autumn becomes golden again with crimson trees and fall flowers, winter returns with a crisp blanket of snow, and spring is fresh with a warm rain and budding flowers. Summer once more is a sweet time of the year. You are beginning to see that there is a rhythm in the seasons and even in your own life there is some return to a routine and a new way of living.

Priorities may change and those things that were so important before now have little value in your life. The important things may revolve around different people and interests that have grown from a new perspective.

There are many positive things that have evolved from that tragic day when your child died. You see in your other children a new sense of caring for others. You notice that people speak to you about a friend of a friend who has lost a child and ask you to please help. You have a different way of looking at life and even a visit to the cemetery can be more calming and not as painful as it once was.

You may find you no longer have time to suffer fools because you have other things that demand your attention.

You realize that every day is precious and should not be wasted.

You realize that death has become the touchstone in your life - you feel that you have seen the worst and experienced the worst, and now you can carry on.

You will never forget, but you will experience healing ... grief has become your spiritual watershed.

You have to make your choices and you have to allow yourself the time and the space to recover so that you can grow. There will be bad days when you simply cannot function, but these will become fewer as the years pass.

There will be moments when you can't make a decision and you question everything you do, but this too shall pass and you will return to your own confidence.

There is hope and there is life after the death of a child - but it will be different, more meaningful in a way that could not have been understood before. You may be more sensitive to others, more judgmental, and you may avoid those who are consumed by senseless pursuits.

You do realize that to everything under the sun, there is a season. You may not like what your season has brought to you, but you come to realize that there will still be time for joy and happiness.

And, there is thanksgiving that you had your child, although it was for such a short time.

You know only too well that the physical pain of bringing forth life, although it can be excruciating, is nothing compared with the emotional agony of seeing life taken away.

And, you realize that your touchstone is your own and no one else can ever fully appreciate it.

You realize that there are many wonderful people out there who will help if you will let them. You realize that you can help others now, since you have been through the worst of all experiences.

You may find that through an organization such as Bereaved Families of Ontario there is tremendous healing, not just in tears, but also in laughter and joy and working with one another.

At some point, when you are ready, you will say farewell to your sorrow - to the deep, cutting sorrow that has had its grip on your being since the day your child died. You will greet the morning once again, and know there is peace.

And, although the child is not physically with you, you do know that the child is indeed a part of your life and your soul forever, and is indeed in your heart and *in your thoughts*.

... and a time to every purpose under the heaven.

In My Thoughts

ACKNOWLEDGMENTS

Special thanks to Margaret McGovern, Executive Director, Bereaved Families of Ontario, Metropolitan Toronto, who has worked so hard to see this book come to life.

Thanks to Corrie Fraser who has coordinated funding of this project.

Thanks to Pamela Erlichman who generously donated her professional editorial services.

Thanks to John Klich for his computer expertise.

Thanks to the following who reviewed the manuscript:

Stan Buda
Chairman, B.S.B. Canada Inc.

Stephen Fleming, Ph.D.

Christine Littlefield, Ph.D., C. Psych.

Barbara Powell
Chair, Parental Committee, BFO

Marie Tunbridge, B.A.

David Wright, B.A., M. Div.

For more information on Bereaved Families of Ontario, Metropolitan Toronto, please call or write ...

Bereaved Families of Ontario, Metropolitan Toronto
214 Merton Street, Suite 204
Toronto, Ontario, M4S 1A6
(416) 440-0290

Barbara Klich is a journalist who has worked as a broadcaster, writer, phone-in show host, and television reporter. She and her husband Ted, a Management Consultant, live in Toronto.

In My Thoughts